5

Parts of Tow Trucks

Tow trucks have radios.

A call on the radio tells

a tow truck driver

where help is needed.

Pebble™ Plus

Mighty Machines

Tow Trucks

by Terri DeGezelle

Consulting Editor: Gail Saunders-Smith, PhD

Consultant: Jeff Hunter
Executive Director
California Tow Truck Association

Capstone
press

Mankato, Minnesota

Pebble Plus is published by Capstone Press,
151 Good Counsel Drive, P.O. Box 669, Mankato, Minnesota 56002.
www.capstonepress.com

1 2 3 4 5 6 11 10 09 08 07 06

Library of Congress Cataloging-in-Publication Data
DeGezelle, Terri, 1955–
    Tow trucks / by Terri DeGezelle.
    p. cm.—(Pebble plus. Mighty machines)
    Summary: "Simple text and photographs present tow trucks, their parts, and their jobs"—Provided by
publisher.
    Includes bibliographical references and index.
    ISBN-13: 978-0-7368-5359-0 (hardcover)
    ISBN-10: 0-7368-5359-6 (hardcover)
    ISBN-13: 978-0-7368-6908-9 (softcover pbk.)
    ISBN-10: 0-7368-6908-5 (softcover pbk.)
    1. Wreckers (Vehicles)—Juvenile literature. 2. Automobiles—Towing—Juvenile literature. I. Title. II. Series.
TL230.5.W74D44 2006
629.225—dc22   2005021608

Editorial Credits
Martha E. H. Rustad, editor; Molly Nei, set designer; Ted Williams, book designer;
    Wanda Winch, photo researcher; Scott Thoms, photo editor

Photo Credits
Capstone Press/Karon Dubke, cover, 1, 4–5, 7, 9, 10–11, 15, 20–21; Corbis/Gunter Marx, 18–19; Peter Arnold,
Inc./Hartmut Schwarzbach, 17; UNICORN Stock Photos/Mark E. Gibson, 12–13

The author thanks Dick Longenecker, Heavy Equipment Operator, Local Union 49er, for his assistance with this
book. Pebble Plus thanks All American Towing of Mankato, Minnesota for assistance with photo shoots.

Note to Parents and Teachers

The Mighty Machines set supports national standards related to science, technology, and
society. This book describes and illustrates tow trucks. The images support early readers
in understanding the text. The repetition of words and phrases helps early readers learn
new words. This book also introduces early readers to subject-specific vocabulary words,
which are defined in the Glossary section. Early readers may need assistance to read
some words and to use the Table of Contents, Glossary, Read More, Internet Sites, and
Index sections of the book.

Table of Contents

A Tow Truck's Job

Tow trucks move
broken cars.
Tow trucks pull cars
to repair shops to be fixed.

radio

Tow trucks have
lights that flash.
The lights warn
other drivers to be careful
around tow trucks.

lights

Tow trucks have wheel lifts.

The wheel lift raises

the front wheels

of a broken car.

wheel lift

Tow trucks have booms
that stretch out.

Booms help lift big trucks
that have tipped over.

What Tow Trucks Do

Tow trucks carry tools
for changing tires
and fixing cars.

Tow trucks move broken cars
off the road.
Then traffic can pass by
on the road.

Tow trucks pull
all kinds of vehicles.
They even tow big trucks.

19

Mighty Tow Trucks

Tow trucks help people
with broken cars.
Tow trucks are
mighty machines.

Glossary

boom—a long metal arm that sticks out from a tow truck

flash—to blink on and off

radio—a tool, similar to a walkie-talkie, used to send and receive messages

tow—to pull something

traffic—cars and trucks moving along a road

warn—to tell people about danger

wheel lift—a metal bar on a tow truck that is shaped like the letter T; a wheel lift fits under a car's wheels and lifts them up.

Read More

Schaefer, Lola M. *Tow Trucks.* Bridgestone Books: The Transportation Library. Mankato, Minn.: Capstone Press, 2000.

Steele, Michael Anthony. *I'm a Great Big Tow Truck!* New York: Scholastic, 2003.

Internet Sites

FactHound offers a safe, fun way to find Internet sites related to this book. All of the sites on FactHound have been researched by our staff.

Here's how:

1. Visit *www.facthound.com*

2. Type in this special code **0736853596** for age-appropriate sites. Or enter a search word related to this book for a more general search.

3. Click on the **Fetch It** button.

FactHound will fetch the best sites for you!

Index

Word Count: 132
Grade: 1
Early-Intervention Level: 16